I AM JOSEPH

Evelyn F. Suarez

Unless otherwise indicated, all Scripture quotations are taken from The ESV©Bible 2001(The Holy Bible, English Standard Version®), copyright © 2001 by Crossway, a publishing ministry of Good News Publishers. Used by permission. All rights reserved

Copyright © 2025 Evelyn F Suarez
All rights reserved
ISBN- 979-8-218-68364-1

"But the Lord was with Joseph and showed him steadfast love and gave him favor in the sight of the keeper of the prison…" Genesis 39:21a
"…because the Lord was with him. And whatever he did, the Lord made it succeed." Genesis 39:23b

Table of Contents

Chapter 1	The Beginning	7
Chapter 2	Enter Joseph	12
Chapter 3	Hope Dashed	16
Chapter 4	This Is A Test	20
Chapter 5	Big Moment	22
Chapter 6	The Encounter	25
Chapter 7	Unexpected Pleasantries	28
Chapter 8	Confrontation	31
Chapter 9	The Big Reveal	33
Chapter 10	Reunion & A Final Goodbye	36
Chapter 11	Surprise Ending & Kindness	38
Chapter 12	The Gist Of The Matter	40

ONE

The Beginning

Are you Joseph? Have you ever faced challenges and hardships that left you crushed? Have you ever been hated to the point of betrayal? Have you ever been smeared and accused of something you never did? After the accusation, have you felt the abandonment of those you thought had your back? Did everyone leave when you needed them the most? Have you ever cried for justice and only heard silence? If so, you may be Joseph.

Many who read Joseph's story get teary-eyed or even cry. It is a compelling account of jealousy, envy, betrayal, injustice, and eventual triumph through integrity, forgiveness, and mercy in one man's life. Its inspiration evokes raw faith and hope in those facing difficult circumstances to a place of restoration and renewal.

Joseph's story begins in Genesis, chapter 37. However, it would be beneficial to delve into his predecessors.

According to the book of Genesis, Joseph's father, Jacob, came from the lineage of Abraham. God had called Abraham out of his country and his father's house and led him to a new land that he would own. He made a covenant with Abraham that his descendants would be like the number of stars that filled the night sky, and kings would come from him. God promised that Abraham would be a blessing and that his name would be great. Although Abraham was a wealthy and prosperous man, he faced many adversities. His son Isaac had a similar experience. "Many are the afflictions of the righteous, but the Lord delivers him out of them all." (Psalm 34:19 ESV) The common denominator was their faith in God. They pioneered a new lifestyle that depended on walking into the unknown by an unseen hand. 2 Corinthians 5:7- "for we walk by faith, not by sight." Habakkuk 2:4b- "But the righteous shall live by his faith." God's promises hinged on their faith and obedience. As it turned out, they struggled due to their imperfect nature, as we all do. But God, faithful in His love and mercy, brought them through every trial and test, fulfilling His purposes through them.

It is worth mentioning the following. Isaac and his wife Rebecca had twin sons, Esau and Jacob. While pregnant, Rebecca felt so much movement within her that she prayed to God to clarify what was happening. God revealed that she was carrying two nations in her womb and that the older would serve the younger. The scriptures confirm that Jacob's hand was upon Esau's heel as they were born. Was it possible that each one was trying to exit first? Did Esau push through, leaving Jacob grasping at his heel in a final attempt to claim firstborn status? This act denoted competitiveness between the brothers. Jacob means supplanter and cheater, and he lived up to his name and, in due time, reaped many consequences as a result. Over time, it became clear that a contentious family had developed due to their parents' favoritism and would be a common theme within their own families over time. Each son's personality became clear as they grew. Esau was a hunter. Jacob preferred staying at home, tending to his father's flocks. And so it was that Isaac favored Esau, the firstborn, partly because of Esau's famous venison stew that he loved to eat. On the other hand, Rebecca favored Jacob, perhaps because he was at home and helped her when necessary.

The title of firstborn came with many benefits, including receiving a more significant inheritance than other siblings. At one point, when Esau arrived home after a day of hunting, he came upon Jacob, who had prepared a stew that was too good to pass up. Esau, tired and hungry, asked for a plate of it. Jacob saw the opportunity to ask him to sell him his birthright in exchange. In his intense desire to eat, Esau carelessly agreed without much thought. He thought Jacob was joking with him. With time, he discovered that this was not the case.

Many years later, Isaac, already aged and blind, sensed he was nearing the end of his days. He called Esau to prepare some venison stew. After enjoying that meal, Isaac promised to bless him with the firstborn blessing. Unbeknownst to Isaac, Rebecca overheard Isaac's mandate to Esau. After Esau left to fulfill his task, she devised a plan to divert the firstborn blessing to Jacob. She quickly called Jacob to relay the scheme. At first, he protested for fear of exposure, but then he relented and joined to deceive his father. Jacob secured the firstborn blessing with precision and careful effort by manipulating his father. That deception was something that I'm sure he deeply regretted for years to come. Esau returned and prepared the venison for his father. When he approached his father to present the stew, Isaac questioned who he was because he had already blessed Esau. It was then that they discovered what his brother Jacob had done. Enraged with hatred, Esau swore he would kill Jacob after his father's death. Upon hearing this, Rebecca convinced Isaac to send Jacob away to her homeland to marry, to protect him from his brother's intentions to kill him for his deception. Sadly, Rebecca's determination to "help" God's prophecy that Jacob would be master over his brother backfired miserably. It brought much sorrow and heartache for them all. The trust was lost because of the deception she and Jacob had conspired against Isaac and Esau. It would be a long time before Esau would feel anything but betrayed by his own family.

Esau struggled as the firstborn. It seemed that anything he did was not good enough. Rebekah did not accept the many women Esau married from the neighboring nations. When he saw that his parents sent Jacob to his mother's land to marry someone suitable, he married a woman from his uncle Ishmael's family. The desire to please his parents was challenging, and his only resort was to move on and build his life elsewhere. This story had a divine purpose that would come to fruition, regardless of the many mistakes committed by the main characters. Despite their faults and imperfections, God saw fit to use these individuals to carry out His purposes.

Jacob left home and headed east toward his mom's hometown. Along the way, he dreamed of a staircase reaching Heaven, and he saw angels ascending and descending upon it. The Lord appeared to Jacob and repeated His promise He made to Abraham that his offspring would be like the dust of the earth, and all the world's families would be blessed through him and his offspring. God promised His presence would be with him wherever he went, bringing him back to this land. Jacob could trust that the Lord would fulfill His promises. Jacob woke from this dream in awe and promised God that if He would bless him, provide for his needs, and return him home in peace, then the Lord would be his God, and he would return a tenth of all that God would give Jacob back to Him.

Interestingly, despite all his failures, God still stood by his side and led him to his destiny as one of the Jewish nation's patriarchs and of the lineage through which the promised Messiah would come. Since the fall of Adam and Eve, this God of mercy and grace knew of man's sinful nature and propensity to miss the mark. But He also knew that Jacob had a teachable heart. Although Isaac and Rebekah were godly parents to Jacob and Esau, some undesirable qualities remained that they passed on to them. Both parents favored one boy in particular. This favoritism fueled a comparison and competition that nearly destroyed them, to the point that Esau wanted to murder Jacob.

Like his grandfather Abraham, God separated Jacob from his family and allowed him to head to another land to begin pruning Jacob. He grew up and had outgrown this territory. With instructions from his father, Isaac, Jacob returned to his mother's homeland.

When he arrived in a particular field in Haran, flocks of sheep were gathered at a well, waiting to be watered. He asked the shepherds where they were from and if they knew of Laban (his uncle). They said they were from Haran, and they knew Laban. They said he was well and directed Jacob's attention to Rachel, Laban's daughter, who arrived with her father's flocks. Upon seeing Rachel, something peculiar in Jacob occurred. He suggested to the shepherds that they water their flocks and return them to their pasture. He wanted them out of there. They replied they could not. All the flocks needed to be gathered to remove the stone from the mouth of the well. Why did Jacob want them to take care of their flocks and get out of there?

Because of Rachel. He felt something for her, and I believe he did not want the shepherds to see his expression of love for her. As Rachel arrived with her father's sheep, Jacob at once removed the heavy stone and watered his uncle's flocks. Then he greeted Rachel with a kiss. It says Jacob raised his voice and wept. I believe Jacob had fallen madly in love with Rachel. He knew immediately in his heart that she was the one he wanted to marry. He then introduced himself as Rebekah's son, who happened to be her father's sister. Rachel ran back home to let her father know. Laban arrived, greeted Jacob with affection, and took him home. They caught up on all that had happened through the years. Jacob remained with him for a month. As a form of payment for living there, Jacob made himself available to help his uncle with whatever needed tending. After a month, Laban asked Jacob what he should pay him, seeing that, although they were related, Jacob deserved wages. The earnings Laban provided Jacob were in the form of marriage. Laban had two daughters: Leah, the older daughter, and Rachel, the younger. Since Jacob had already fallen in love with Rachel, he offered to work seven years for Rachel's hand in marriage. Laban accepted and even said he preferred to give her to Jacob over any other man. So, Jacob worked for seven years for Rachel, and it seemed like a few days to him because of his love for her. Jacob genuinely loved Rachel.

After completing the seven years, Jacob approached Laban to receive "his wages," his promised bride, Rachel. Laban prepared a marriage feast and gathered the family and friends for this special occasion. After the festivities had ended, Laban took Leah, instead of Rachel, to Jacob. It was nighttime, and the custom was that the bride was veiled; therefore, it was difficult for Jacob to see her. Laban also, as was the custom, gave Leah a maid, Zilpah. The following day, upon awakening, Jacob realized he had slept with Leah and confronted Laban and asked him why he had deceived him like that. He questioned Laban why he had given him Leah instead of Rachel, if he had agreed to work for Rachel, not Leah. Laban said that in their custom, the younger was not allowed to marry before the older. He would need to finish the marriage week for Leah, and then he would receive Rachel. He would have to fulfill another seven years to complete his wages. So, Jacob complied and fulfilled the marriage week and obtained Rachel as well. She was given a maid named Bilhah as well. Jacob loved Rachel and favored her over her sister, Leah. Because of this slight, Leah conceived children, but Rachel was barren. There was more to the reason why Rachel could not conceive at that time. I will explain briefly.

What followed was the growth of Jacob's family through four wives. It was endless years of comparison and competition, jealousy, and manipulation. Leah felt empowered, seeing that she had an advantage over her sister in childbearing. Rachel felt the sting of barrenness and even told Jacob to give her children, or she would die. Such was the burden of motherhood that many women carried in that culture. Barren women were looked down upon. Seeing the years pass and having no hope of ever having a child, Rachel resorted to giving her maid to Jacob to try to have a child through their union. Her maid succeeded, and Leah, in a competitive mode, offered her own maid to Jacob to gain more children. It was a back-and-forth between the two. At times, I imagine the level of discord and rivalry must have taken its toll on Jacob.

Reflecting on his circumstances, Jacob may have understood two indisputable reasons for his predicament. One was reaping what he had sown in his earlier years. Looking back, he may have recalled his deception towards his father and brother. Now, his father-in-law had dealt him with a similar hand. The second is related to the hardships a person endures because of the great purpose tied to their life. Jacob was one of the patriarchs who had received a great promise from God. That promise brought with it much suffering and trouble. It is filled with struggles, difficulties, and trials that the average person will not have to face. It is years of striving and persistence. It is patience beyond the norm. Many times, it is the "not knowing" that stretches faith to its breaking point. Where one desperately wants to give up because there is no relief in sight. The voice that keeps pestering and hurling a barrage of despair and relentlessly challenges the tiny flicker of hope that remains. And in that season, or years of testing, strength is developed. The resistance to giving up develops a rock-like muscle of stability and resilience. The trials that follow seem not so significant. The response to the voice of despair is "not going to give up," "I've come too far to turn back," and "this discomfort can't compare to obtaining the promise."

The fact that Rachel was barren at first has significance. Rachel was Jacob's chosen wife, and Leah was positioned into the relationship by deception. Although God had mercy and allowed Leah to bear more children, that is not a sign that she was the one chosen for Jacob. Jacob loved

Rachel, and God reserved a unique gift for her: Joseph. She eventually had two sons, the two youngest, Joseph and Benjamin. Their father loved them supremely. They were the only ones out of the twelve who were obedient and pure in heart. The scriptures state that Jacob's sons by Leah and the two handmaidens were a source of heartache and stress. There was constant rivalry and many moments of vengeful acts that they committed. Their spirits were not godly. Therefore, God closed Rachel's womb for a time because Joseph's birth was determined for a specific time to coincide with the great calling he would fulfill.

To further expound on this matter of a God-chosen spouse, in 1 Samuel 1, we have the case of Hannah and Peninah, the two wives of Elkanah. Hannah was the chosen one, greatly loved by her husband, Elkanah, and she was barren. Peninah had children and spent her time mocking Hannah. But God turned it around because the child Hannah eventually bore was none other than Samuel, one of the greatest prophets of Israel. She went on to bear five more children. On a side note, we can see polygamy will never work. I rest my case.

At first, his uncle Laban was fascinated with Jacob and offered him a job. However, Laban's true character came out after many years of working for him. Jacob dismissed the first red flag when he was fooled into marrying Leah first before Rachel. The eldest marrying first was, according to their tradition, explained by Laban. Eventually, Jacob realized that Laban was a cheater and manipulator. This realization triggered in him the necessary changes to lead a godly life. Jacob's refusal to compromise his character with his uncle and father-in-law brought much discord and contention. As Jacob increased in wealth and prosperity, Laban's sons began accusing Jacob of stealing from his uncle's flocks. They did not know it was a sign of the favor of God upon his life. His uprightness began to reap blessings upon blessings. Again, we can see Jacob had outgrown living in his uncle's house. It was time to move, and God instructed him to return to his homeland. He packed up his possessions, gathered his wives, children, servants, and flocks, and began returning home. Jacob was not the same man who, years before, had left his father's home. He was no longer a cheater nor a supplanter. He was walking in his purpose, following God's guidance, and leaving a legacy of faith and trust in the Almighty.

He strived to instill these values in his children. With twelve sons, Joseph seemed to be the only one listening and receiving his father's teachings. Observing his other sons' behaviors led Jacob to conclude that Joseph was the best candidate to take the lead. All that he invested in Joseph would be the best decision he could have made concerning the blessing upon his descendants.

A challenging and sad moment occurred with the birth of his twelfth son. Rachel did not survive childbirth and died soon after Benjamin was born. Jacob was grief-stricken. Over time, his two youngest sons became his comfort.

TWO

ENTER JOSEPH

Joseph's story commences in Genesis 37.. The son of Rachel, Jacob's chosen wife, Joseph, was born during Jacob's older years, earning him a special place in Jacob's life. The verses in chapter 37 give us a glimpse into the dynamics of this unusual family. As the eleventh son, finding his place among his half-brothers must have been challenging. Joseph had his share of tasks to fulfill, one being a shepherd. By seventeen, Jacob had chosen Joseph to track his brothers while in the field with them. It did not go well for Joseph. The fact was that Jacob's older sons were problematic, unruly, and disrespectful. What a predicament to find himself in. His truthfulness about his brothers' poor behavior created hatred towards him. It was not as if he deliberately tried to get them in trouble. Although he chose the correct route in his dealings with them, they were not having it. If Jacob had any idea the heavy responsibility he had placed on Joseph would have repercussions, but he did not show it. He thrust Joseph into a leadership role and expected his older sons to respect him. As if that was not enough, he designed a multi-colored special robe for Joseph. It was a reward for his faithfulness in his duties. It was also an identifier. It identified Joseph as specially selected by God for a specific purpose. His brothers thought otherwise; they did not believe Joseph deserved such an honor, making them extremely angry. Communication between them came to a halt. They would not speak peacefully to him. The hostile, toxic atmosphere continued to brew.

One day, Joseph told his brothers about a dream he had. In the dream, he saw them binding sheaves in the field. Then his sheaf rose straight up, and his brother's sheaves gathered around and bowed to his sheaf. To say they were not thrilled is an understatement. They asked, "Are you indeed to reign over us? Or are you indeed to rule over us?" Their hate continued to increase on account of his dreams and his words" (Gen 37:8). "And Jesus said to them, "A prophet is not without honor, except in his hometown and among his relatives and in his own household" (Mark 6:4).

They became even more outraged with his next dream. He dreamt that the sun, the moon, and eleven stars bowed to him. When his father heard it, he rebuked Joseph. "But when he told his father and his brothers about it, his father rebuked him and said to him, "What is this dream that you have dreamed? Shall I and your mother and your brothers indeed come to bow ourselves to the ground before you?" (Gen 37:10). His brother's jealousy reached the breaking point. But Jacob quietly pondered these dreams as a sort of revelation. Poor Joseph! His dreams were not appreciated, nor could he ever be celebrated among his own. "I have become a stranger to my brothers, an alien to my mother's sons" (Ps 69:8).

At this point, it became clear that Jacob's older sons felt threatened by Joseph. All ten followed the standard behavior patterns they had set. Joseph, on the other hand, did not adapt to their mindset. He obeyed their father, and that was unsettling to them. They tried different means to discourage, intimidate, and belittle him. His will to do right outweighed the temptation to fit in. It was an unfortunate scene to behold. How sad to see Joseph targeted as the problem. They made him feel unwelcome among his family members. At the same time, I see how God revealed the difference in character between Joseph and his brothers—time would play a hand in Joseph's destiny. As uncomfortable and painful as it was to experience being the black sheep of the family, it was necessary. The contrast had to be clear.

Joseph intimidated ten men. They saw in him a level of goodness that they could not understand, and it scared them. They knew it was a sign of more extraordinary things in store for Joseph. They conversed among themselves about him, and all they could do was point out what was wrong with Joseph. They laughed and mocked him. Things began to take a darker tone. Their feelings toward him went from anger and jealousy to hate. They wanted to end all this discomfort by putting an end to Joseph's life. In a matter of days, they would try it. "My brothers are treacherous as a torrent-bed, as torrential streams that pass away" (Job 6:15).

It is an indisputable fact that Joseph was abused by his brothers. As is the case with many trauma survivors, the environment one is raised in becomes the norm. Because of the mistreatment Joseph received, he did not expect any kindness from them after many years. Each day was like any other in his mind. What made it bearable for Joseph was having his father around to provide comfort and knowing he loved him.

In verse 12 of chapter 37, his brothers took their father's flocks to pasture them near the city of Shechem. As was the custom, Jacob sent Joseph to check on them. They were supposed to be near Shechem, and that is where Joseph headed. Upon arriving there, his brothers were nowhere to be found. A man saw Joseph wandering around and asked him what he was looking for. He replied that he was searching for his brothers and asked if he knew where they had gone. The man said he had overheard them say they would go to Dothan. Interestingly, this man happened to hear Joseph's brothers and then directed him to where they were. Was this an angelic intervention?

Would it be possible his brothers knew he would come to check on them and decided to go somewhere else to throw him off their trail? They hoped he would get lost forever, never to be seen again. Whether that was the case or not, it did not prevent him from finding them. At a distance, they could make out their younger brother heading towards their camp. They could hear him calling out to them, "Brothers!" It irritated them.

Again, poor Joseph! Why did he always have to be outnumbered? Why did he always have to face off against his brothers? Why was there no one to support him when he needed it? Would this be his fate forever? As he neared the camp, his eyes caught a glimpse of the hatred in his brother's eyes. It was like being surrounded by a pack of wolves. They were ready to pounce on him. His stomach churned because of the uneasiness he sensed. His gut told him something was terribly off this time, and he was right. Before he was even near them, they had already decided that they would kill him and throw him into a pit. They would tell their father that a fierce animal had devoured him to cover their crime. No one would know since there were no surveillance cameras. Then, the oldest, Ruben, told them not to kill him but to throw him into one of the pits. He planned on secretly rescuing him and getting him back home. Upon entering the camp, Joseph's brothers grabbed him, removed his special robe, and threw him into a pit. Fortunately, it held no water.

"The Lord will make righteous people safe. He will take care of them in times of trouble. The Lord helps them. He saves them from wicked people. He keeps them safe because they turn to him for help" (Ps 37:39-40).

There may not have been any surveillance cameras, but there was One who was watching what these men were planning to do. Their mistreatment was only allowed up to a certain point. They wanted to see what would become of Joseph's dreams if they ended his life. God used the oldest brother to rescue Joseph. They did not understand that Joseph did not author his dreams. God was the originator. They had been fighting Someone too powerful to beat.

They removed his coat as if to do away with his identity. They thought that his coat was what distinguished Joseph from them, and they believed that removing it would remove his purpose. They could remove his coat, but not the calling and purpose for Joseph's life.

Their carelessness towards Joseph became more noticeable as they sat down to eat. Joseph was like a captive prey in a pit, out of view but close enough to taunt and keep a watchful eye on. They had their fill of jokes at Joseph's expense, unaware that their taunts would haunt them in years to come. As they looked up, they noticed a caravan of Ishmaelites. These were traders heading to Egypt with items such as gum, balm, and myrrh. They looked at one another as if to say, "Are you thinking what I'm thinking?" Judah broke the silence and expressed their thoughts. "What will we gain if we kill him and try to hide it? Let us sell him to the Ishmaelites; we will not be guilty of shedding his blood. After all, he is our brother." They all agreed and put the plan into action. I will mention that the eldest brother, Ruben, was not present and was not part of the transactional committee. They pulled Joseph out of the pit and presented him to the traders, who had good eyes to see the value of this young man; they could quickly sell him in Egypt. All it took was twenty shekels of silver to get rid of Joseph and send him to Egypt.

Ruben arrived afterward, and upon discovering Joseph was gone, his only concern was how he would face their father with the news. Never mind Joseph's well-being. I can only imagine how Joseph must have felt. As he was being pulled out of the pit, he felt some hope that his brothers had reconsidered their treatment of him. The horror of realizing they had pulled him out only to sell him to some traders was too much. Now, he would never see his father or home again. The pain and sorrow he felt had to be overwhelming, and now, he had to adjust to a new world and life in Egypt. If this were his treatment within his family, what could he expect in a foreign country as a prisoner? Life had suddenly taken a turn for the worse.

In response to Ruben's concerns about their father's inquiry about Joseph, the brothers decided to cover Joseph's robe in goat blood. They hoped this would be sufficient evidence that a fierce animal had killed Joseph and put an end to all mention of Joseph. Presented with proof of Joseph's demise, Jacob tore his clothing and put on sackcloth for many days as he mourned his son. He refused comfort from the rest of the family and spent his days grieving for Joseph. After the loss of Rachel, his great love, Jacob now had to suffer another significant loss, his beloved Joseph. How could he go on? His sons knew he would grieve, but they never imagined the extent of his sorrow. Now, they would never hear the end of his weeping over Joseph, whom they despised. Meanwhile, Joseph was taken to Egypt and promptly sold to Potiphar, one of Pharaoh's officers and a guard captain.

THREE

HOPE DASHED

Chapter 38 recounts a moment in Judah's life that tested his character. Despite the negative aspects of that circumstance, Judah began to stand out as a leader among his brothers, as we will see further.

We will continue with chapter 39. As stated, Joseph began his journey to Egypt, an unfamiliar land. Back at home, Joseph had his father as a guide, instructor, and the occasional ear as a confidant. Now, all that he had learned up to this point would be tested. "Train up a child in the way he should go; even when he is old, he will not depart from it" (Prov 22:6). One of Jacob's main lessons to Joseph was faith in God. As was his experience in the desert before arriving at his uncle Laban's home, Jacob understood that God was ever-present, all-knowing, and all-powerful. This fundamental truth would prove to be Joseph's enduring comfort and strength.

Upon arriving in Egypt, Joseph was sold to Potiphar, captain, and officer of Pharaoh. In verse two, we read that the Lord was with Joseph. Placing Joseph in this official's home was a calculated move by God. His presence and favor upon Joseph's life brought success in all Joseph did. Over time, Potiphar noticed Joseph's unique qualities and soon made him the administrator of all his household and business dealings. Blessings became abundant when Joseph was promoted to overseeing Potiphar's estate. Everything flourished under Joseph's hands. "The reward for humility and fear of the Lord is riches, honor, and life"(Prov 22:4). "Both riches and honor come from you, and you rule overall. In your hand are power and might, and in your hand, it is to make great and to give strength to all" (1 Chron 29:12). "Wealth and riches are in his house, and his righteousness endures forever" (Ps 112:3). As with every good moment in a story, there is always that sense of imminent threat or spoiling. Just when everything is going well and on the up and up comes that person who provides the pullback.

From a spiritual perspective, it is without saying that the enemy will not remain with his arms crossed, watching a child of God prosper and succeed without opposition. It is mentioned that Joseph's physical appearance and purity were appealing, making him stand out among the many servants in Potiphar's house. The Bible does not mention her name, so we will call her Potiphar's wife, as the Bible refers to her. As time passed, Potiphar's wife looked lustfully upon Joseph. She became brazen by inviting him to sleep with her. Joseph expressed no interest and told her. "But he refused and said to his master's wife, "Behold, because of me, my master has no concern about anything in the house, and he has put everything that he has in my charge. He is not greater in this house than I am, nor has he kept back anything from me except you because you are his wife. How then can I do this great wickedness and sin against God?" (Gen 39:8-9). Potiphar's wife was relentless, and one day, when no one was around, she physically pulled him and tried to force him to engage in sexual relations with her. Joseph ran off, and she stayed with his garment in her hand. She screamed, and when the other servants arrived, she claimed Joseph tried to take advantage of her but ran when she yelled and left his garment. She repeated her story to her husband. As I mentioned earlier, there were no surveillance cameras then, and who would Potiphar believe? His wife, of course. As is clear, Joseph, in goodwill towards Potiphar, kept a professional manner and high work ethic in all his work. This situation exposed both Potiphar's wife and Joseph's characters. What Satan intended at this point was to disgrace Joseph in a scandal. But God used this whole situation to test Joseph's character. Joseph proved himself to be upright and faithful to God. "Many are the afflictions of the righteous, but the Lord delivers him out of them all"(Ps 34:19).

Unfortunately, Potiphar, in a moment of anger, reacted with fury and imprisoned Joseph. From a human standpoint, God seemed unjust. How could he allow Joseph to be falsely accused when he had been faithful in all his dealings? He had been doing so well in Potiphar's house, and now he was criminalized and sent to prison. There was no justice. No legal system existed at that time. It was Potiphar's wife's word against Joseph, a mere foreign servant. There was no opportunity given to Joseph to defend himself. He had done everything right, but it still landed him in a place of despair with no hope of ever being released. The thoughts that may have invaded Joseph's mind must have been countless. It seemed like doing right and being obedient only got Joseph into trouble. First, his brothers and then Potiphar's wife were able to manipulate situations that landed him into incarceration and bondage. What Joseph could not see now was, in each instance, he shined as bright as a star. His light exposed the evilness of his brothers and Potiphar's wife. They stayed evil, but he kept shining brighter. The tears he shed and feelings of unfairness he felt might have taken their toll on Joseph had it not been for God's unfailing love and mercy that unveiled themselves over time in that prison. I can almost hear God telling Joseph- "don't despair; your time at home and in Potiphar's house is up. You are on to more incredible things. Trust me." "I will make you as a light for the nations, that my salvation may reach to the end of the earth" (Is 49:6).

To go to prison without just cause was another plan in God's arsenal of weapons. Satan's eyes were upon Joseph. He had set him up to fail, and, he supposedly had succeeded. In the natural, it looked like a defeat. Now, all who saw him looked upon him with disdain. He was the object of ridicule, mockery, and even hate for his crime. Could it get any worse than this?

Joseph was placed in the royal prison, where the king's prisoners were kept. I find this a level up from the general prison population, and it was, again, a deliberate move by God. Here, he would have contact with the king's officials and exposure. He would have access to information that the general prison population did not. As what happened at Potiphar's house, it did not take long for the prison keeper to notice Joseph's unique qualities. Here again, Joseph was promoted to manager of the prison. He attended to all that pertained to the prisoners, their needs, and daily provisions. God's favor showed itself in Joseph's life, and everything he did prospered. The prison system seemed to run smoothly like never before, and it all began after Joseph arrived. Joseph started to get a clearer picture of something marvelous in his life now. The prison keeper could feel relieved if Joseph were around.

Although the system may have improved, individuals may have eyed Joseph with jealousy and envy. There may have been instigators or haters who tried to disrupt the flow of normality. They knew Joseph was the outsider, and they were right. He was a foreigner who had much to learn: the language, the customs, the culture, and even the religious beliefs, which were a prominent feature of the Egyptian lifestyle. Adapting to a new set of rules was challenging, and he had his moments of discouragement. Not having anyone to unburden himself to must have been disheartening. It was in these moments that Joseph's faith and trust in God deepened. The days continued to pass; each day turned into weeks. The weeks turned into months, and the months turned into years. The daily routine became mundane at times. He had moments where he questioned when he would be released. Why was he still in prison? Would he ever see his father again? At the end of every year, he thought the following year would be the year of his release. But as that year winded down, nothing happened. Joseph was still in the royal prison. Some prisoners were released, but not him. That is when the thoughts of unfairness would strike.

Depression wanted to set in. Fear and anxiety would take a stranglehold on him. But he prayed, and with tears, he would cry out to God for strength. Hope would somehow creep back in, and he had survived another day. It became a rollercoaster of constant emotions and negative thoughts. The cycles continued: he had moments of hope and peace. His strength would be renewed. Then, thoughts of anxiety would well up as he pondered the time that he was enduring an unjust system. It was a constant battle to not feel or think about the unfairness of it all. He could sense that little sneering voice invading him at night as he went to sleep.

Where is God in all this? Why hasn't He done anything for your release? You serve your God faithfully and look at you. You are still here. Your God does not exist. If He does, He does not care about you at all. On and on, the thoughts would come. Sometimes, he felt anger at his brothers as they handled the direction his life had taken. If they had not sold him, he would still be at home. He also felt angry at Potiphar and his wife. After all he had done, serving him faithfully, he did his best to resist her advances. But even that was not enough. Her accusations prevailed against him and now look where he ended up. At times, Joseph thought he would go insane. But he realized over time that he had to cling to God continually for strength, wisdom, comfort, and peace to withstand the years of imprisonment. Like what his father, Jacob, endured for many years while working for his father-in-law, Laban.

As time passed, Joseph developed some friendships among the prisoners. They exchanged stories and he became aware of the hardships many of them had endured as well. Joseph felt compassion for them and was able to offer words of encouragement. It was in those moments that he understood why he was there. God was using him to help the prisoners. He brought them hope and shared his testimony of how God's presence in his life made it all bearable. His dreams helped keep him focused on God's purpose and plan for him. If he replaced the thoughts of fear with faith in God's faithfulness, he felt a peace that passed all understanding. "And the peace of God, which surpasses all understanding, will guard your hearts and your minds in Christ Jesus" (Phil 4:7). "You keep him in perfect peace whose mind is stayed on you because he trusts in you" (Isaiah 26:3).

He reasoned that after coming this far, why would he give up now? Looking back, he remembered the years he had helped tending his father's flocks. His father entrusted him with watching over his brother's work. When he arrived in Egypt and entered service at Potiphar's house, he succeeded as an administrator. After the false accusations by Potiphar's wife landed him in prison, he once again found himself in an administrative position. He noticed a pattern. Although each circumstance he encountered was adverse, he was put in a leadership position. It was all becoming plain that these roles were related to his dreams. In time, whatever God had in store would unfold. Behind the scenes, God was working on this extraordinary story. It was a learning process for Joseph. He had much to see and learn while in a prison environment. It began to dawn on him that he was not to look for a way out of prison but the higher purpose for which he had been chosen.

Along with the mundane came the unexpected. One thing that became clear to Joseph was that anything that annoyed the king would affect the officials within the palace, who then turned on the servants and so forth. His ears became keener to listen to the language and method of address while in the king's court if the need ever arose. It seemed like a lot of pressure, but this experience would lay the framework for his future success.

Whether he knew it or not, he was being carefully observed. As a foreigner, his life was markedly different from the rest of the prisoners. His attitude, conduct, and self-discipline distinguished him from the others, laying the foundation for his promotion. He learned who he could trust and who he could not. God had a way of exposing those around him, and this time was of extreme importance for Joseph. He had to learn when to speak and when to keep silent. Joseph had to know what to say and what not to share. He realized who had ulterior motives and who was pure-hearted. His discernment became sharp due to his closeness with God.

There are things that one will understand based on one's communion with God. He opens his eyes to see what others cannot. God also reveals what is hidden and what is being said in secret. The Kingdom of Darkness may have a bit of access and can try their hand at it. But the purpose of said Kingdom is to steal, kill, and destroy. Therefore, why rely on a deceptive and evil source when you can have the Originator provide the information? You will never go wrong because He is the source of all truth. He will never betray or switch on you. His purpose is to save, bless, and add to your life.

Joseph discovered his purpose while in prison. Each day was another opportunity to sharpen his skills and develop his gifts. He got better at it and enjoyed seeing his work produce and expand. He was feeling more peaceful and a growing desire to help others. These changes occurring in Joseph were all due to God. God's favor began to build up on him to the point that God finally did something to get him to where Joseph was destined to be. He had been in prison for eleven years, and he had arrived for the next season of his life.

FOUR

THIS IS A TEST

About eleven years into Joseph's arrival in Egypt, two of the king's officials, the baker and cupbearer, committed a grave offense against the king. The Pharaoh was angry with them, and they were taken into custody in the royal prison where Joseph was. He was to attend to their needs. One night, the baker and cupbearer each had a dream. The following morning, Joseph noticed their troubled expressions and asked them what the matter was. They replied that they each had a dream but did not know how to interpret it. Joseph invited them to share their dreams and offered reassurance that God would use him to interpret them.

Before continuing the story, I want to highlight Joseph's most outstanding characteristics. It has to do with his integrity. Upon reflecting on his dealings with Potiphar and the prison keeper, Joseph became known as trustworthy, which advanced him into leadership positions. This trait was noticeable throughout his teen years when his father appointed him to watch over his brother's. Jacob could trust Joseph because he had shown honesty and truthfulness, traits his brothers were unwilling to develop. His arrival to Egypt was a continuation of keeping a genuine, truthful, and careful lifestyle. His years in prison did not diminish this mindfulness but became his trademark. The prison keeper felt confident Joseph could manage watching over the necessities of these two official prisoners. This moment was a milestone in Joseph's journey that would catapult him into a place he could only dream of. "Do you see a man skillful in his work? He will stand before kings; he will not stand before obscure men" (Prov 22:29).

The cupbearer shared his dream first. "So the chief cupbearer told his dream to Joseph and said to him, "In my dream, there was a vine before me, and on the vine, there were three branches. As soon as it budded, its blossoms shot forth, and the clusters ripened into grapes. Pharaoh's cup was in my hand, and I took the grapes and pressed them into Pharaoh's cup and placed the cup in Pharaoh's hand" (Gen 40:9-11). According to the text, Joseph had the interpretation at once because it says, then Joseph said to him. It does not say it took a couple of hours, minutes, or days. He had the answer at once. It was a favorable interpretation, filled with hope for the cupbearer. He would leave prison in three days and receive his position back as before. Joseph included a plea to the cupbearer to remember him and speak to the Pharaoh on his behalf to seek his release from prison. He briefly explained the circumstances that caused him to be unjustly imprisoned. Seeing this optimistic interpretation, the baker also related his dream to Joseph. "When the chief baker saw that the interpretation was favorable, he said to Joseph, "I also had a dream: there were three cake baskets on my head, and in the uppermost basket there were all sorts of baked food for Pharaoh, but the birds were eating it out of the basket on my head" (Gen 40:16-17 ESV). I imagine Joseph's face held a solemn expression, and he paused before revealing the interpretation. Unfortunately for the baker, the news was not good. Here again, we see Joseph put to the test. Delivering unwelcome news to a king's official required a level of guts that Joseph had to develop, whether he wanted to or not. A leader must accept the bad, difficult, reasonable, and easy moments since life offers a mixture. The number three prevalent in both dreams meant the timing was the same. As with the cupbearer, the baker's fate would be revealed within three days. The difference was that the baker would be hung and be a meal for the birds. At this point, each had the choice of accepting their fate or skepticism.

The third day arrived, and it was the Pharaoh's birthday. He held a feast for his servants, and in the process, not only was the cupbearer restored to his former position, but the chief baker was hung. Joseph waited and waited, expecting the cupbearer to show some gratitude by speaking on his behalf to the king. Imagine the painful reality as time passed; the cupbearer went his way and forgot Joseph's kindness. How does a person manage not to sink into despair and frustration under such circumstances? Joseph was human, which is understandable if he had gone through such emotions. He did. Somehow, with God's still small voice of encouragement, Joseph continued to face each day with patience and fortitude. "But let patience have its perfect work, that you may be perfect and complete, lacking nothing" James 1:4 (NKJV).

Here, we see maturity in his acceptance of God's purposes and timing. He always had a choice: either give up or keep on going, believing that something greater lay ahead. He had come this far, and there was no going back. He kept kicking despair and frustration to the curb and kept a high-level mindset. He held onto the hope that God would one day offer a way out of this prison. It would occur at the precise divine time. "The smallest family will become a thousand people, and the tiniest group will become a mighty nation. At the right time, I, the Lord, will make it happen " (Is 60:22 New Living Translation).

The fact the cupbearer "forgot" about Joseph can be for several reasons. He was a sort of gatekeeper before the Pharaoh. One reason could be that he saw Joseph as a simple prisoner who had just been lucky in interpreting the dreams. Another could have been that he wanted to be sure that Joseph was what he portrayed: an innocent victim of circumstance. It could be he felt fear and intimidation. Fear that Joseph was a more extraordinary individual with potential and would end up in a higher position than him. Whatever it was, it prolonged Joseph's time of testing. Whether done intentionally on the cupbearers' part or not, it did not cancel God's promise for Joseph's elevation. God knew what He was doing. Ultimately, God decided to keep Joseph a bit longer. There were a few tweaks that had to be made before the promise could be fulfilled. Joseph was ready, but the timing had to be exactly right. The event that called for Joseph had not arrived yet. And as disappointing as it may have been for him, the wait was indeed worth it.

FIVE

BIG MOMENT

Life continued for Joseph in the Egyptian prison. Two years had passed since his encounter with the chief cupbearer and chief baker. During this period, nothing new occurred. Each day was a routine. Unknown to him, something supernatural had been dispatched from Heaven and received by the king in the form of two dreams.

Genesis 41:1-7 states- "After two whole years, Pharaoh dreamed that he was standing by the Nile, and behold, there came up out of the Nile seven cows, attractive and plump, and they fed in the reed grass. And behold, seven other cows, ugly and thin, came up out of the Nile after them, and stood by the other cows on the bank of the Nile. And the ugly, thin cows ate up the seven attractive, plump cows. And Pharaoh awoke. And he fell asleep and dreamed a second time. And behold, seven ears of grain, plump and good, were growing on one stalk. And behold, after them sprouted seven ears, thin and blighted by the east wind. And the thin ears swallowed up the seven plump, full ears. And Pharaoh awoke, and behold, it was a dream." Pharaoh woke up troubled by these two dreams he had in succession. That morning, he called for all his magicians and wise men to tell them the dreams to see if they could interpret them. As hard as they tried, no one could interpret the dreams. No one, not even Pharaoh's "wise men," could provide an interpretation for his dreams.

It was an aha moment for the chief cupbearer as a sudden memory compelled him to approach the king with the name of someone who could interpret his dream. He explained how he and the chief baker had been imprisoned for an offense against the Pharaoh two years earlier. Each had a dream, but they were unable to interpret it. One of the prisoners there, a young Hebrew who served the captain of the guard, had been able to interpret their dreams. The cupbearer was restored to his position while the baker was hung just as the young Hebrew had said. The Pharaoh, upon hearing the cupbearer's testimony, sent for this Hebrew by the name of Joseph.

In one day, within minutes, Joseph's whole life took an unexpected turn for the better. He was brought before the king after a shave, a bath, and a change of clothes. At this moment, we see the beginning of the fulfillment of the dream Joseph had received over thirteen years earlier. A bit nervous and with wonderment, he was about to use his God-given gift in the king's court before all the officials and the Pharaoh himself.

As Pharaoh watched this prisoner who stood before him, he was intrigued. None of his wise advisors, whom he trusted, had been able to interpret his dreams. Who was this man who showed evidence of superior knowledge of dream interpretation? Although the scriptures do not mention it, I can assume Pharaoh inquired more about Joseph: where he was from and how long he had been in prison. Joseph assured the Pharaoh that God would provide the correct interpretation.

Pharaoh then recounted his dreams to Joseph. Upon hearing the dreams, Joseph explained their meaning with precision. Genesis 41:25-32- "Then Joseph said to Pharaoh, "The dreams of Pharaoh are one; God has revealed to Pharaoh what he is about to do. The seven good cows are seven years, and the seven good ears are seven years; the dreams are one. The seven lean and ugly cows that came up after them are seven years, and the seven empty ears blighted by the east wind are also seven years of famine. It is as I told Pharaoh; God has shown to Pharaoh what he is about to do. There will come seven years of great plenty throughout all the land of Egypt, but after them there will arise seven years of famine, and all the plenty will be forgotten in the land of Egypt. The famine will consume the land, and the plenty will be unknown in the land by reason of the famine that will follow, for it will be very severe. And the doubling of Pharaoh's dream means that the thing is fixed by God, and God will shortly bring it about."

With the interpretation came a word of wisdom from God to appoint a wise man to oversee food gathering during the seven years of abundance. This mighty undertaking would be a means to provide the populace during the seven years of famine that would follow. Genesis 41:33-36- "Now therefore let Pharaoh select a discerning and wise man, and set him over the land of Egypt. Let Pharaoh proceed to appoint overseers over the land and take one-fifth of the produce of the land of Egypt during the seven plentiful years. And let them gather all the food of these good years that are coming and store up grain under the authority of Pharaoh for food in the cities, and let them keep it. That food shall be a reserve for the land against the seven years of famine that are to occur in the land of Egypt, so that the land may not perish through the famine."" As in the story of Esther, where she had entered as queen into the Persian kingdom precisely to save her people, Joseph arrives on the scene at the precipice of a worldwide crisis. What better-qualified man than the one standing before the Pharaoh for the job of overseer or the vizier? He would be the governor of Egypt, second only to the king. He would command the whole Egyptian economy, welfare, and military.

Pharaoh turned to his advisers and asked who else besides Joseph could manage such an immense task. You could hear a pin drop. All, in silent agreement, stared at their new governor. There was a Godly favor upon Joseph that they all could discern. Although they may have felt anxiety about the future, they felt relief that they had a divine connection through Joseph. In one day, Joseph stepped out of a prison into the royal palace by the hand and providence of God. This unexpected, unanticipated turn of events surprised everyone, including Joseph.

Upon hearing the interpretation of his dream and the counsel for preparing to face the eventual crisis, Pharaoh appointed Joseph as the new governor of Egypt. Joseph received the king's signet ring, garments of fine linen, and a gold chain about his neck. He was prescribed the second chariot, and all were made to bow before him throughout the kingdom. On that day, Pharaoh granted Joseph second-in-command authority in Egypt. Joseph's name was changed to Zaphenath-paneah. Some have interpreted it to mean "he who is revealed by God" or "revealer of secrets." Another interpretation is "savior of the world." He also married Asenath, the daughter of Potiphera, priest of On, by the king's choice. The range of emotions that Joseph must have experienced was overwhelming. He was thirty years old when he began his service before the king of Egypt.

"For you, O God, have tested us; you have tried us as silver is tried. You brought us into the net; you laid a crushing burden on our backs; you let men ride over our heads; we went through fire and through water; yet you have brought us out to a place of abundance" (Psa 66:10-12).

"The reward for humility and fear of the Lord is riches and honor and life" (Prov 22:4).

Upon leaving Pharoah's court, Joseph began inspecting all of Egypt. All of Egypt had begun experiencing an abundance of crops. The fertile land grew grain upon grain. For seven years, Joseph gathered all the grain into huge piles, so much so that he could no longer keep a record. God was faithful to provide such an abundance that would be enough to provide enough food for seven years of worldwide famine. Only God can do that.

During these seven years, two sons were born to Joseph and his wife, Asenath. The firstborn was named Manasseh, for he said, "God has made me forget all my troubles and everyone in my father's family." Joseph called his second son Ephraim, for he said, "God has made me fruitful in this land of my grief." With the naming of each son, Joseph recognized the process God had brought him through healing and restoration, which both allowed him to continue in his great mission in life.

Joseph reflected on all the years of mistreatment, rejection, betrayal, and false accusations. He accepted the role of each stage not as a defeat but as a testimony to God's faithfulness. God had given him his dreams and brought them to fruition. And it was by far more than he could have ever imagined.

Just as he had interpreted Pharoah's dream, the seven years of plenty ended, and the seven years of want or famine began. At first, you could barely tell there was a famine. They experienced plenty in the land of Egypt. But, then the days of rain decreased. As the months passed, the vegetation started to wither and die. Slowly but surely, Egypt began to look like a wasteland. Not only Egypt but the surrounding countries began to experience this dreaded famine. These countries had no idea what lay ahead. The Egyptians had the advantage of having stored up grain during the years of plenty, as Joseph had recommended.

When reality finally hit that they had run out, the populace came before Pharoah, pleading for food. His response revealed the amount of respect and admiration he had for Joseph. Not even Pharoah could handle this crisis. He was so thankful to God for sending someone who knew just what to do and did it so well. He directed the people to go to Joseph and do whatever he told them. The storehouses were opened, and grain was distributed to the people. With time, the famine was so severe worldwide that people from all around came to Egypt to buy grain from Joseph. "He has brought down the mighty from their thrones and exalted those of humble estate;" (Luke 1:52).

SIX

THE ENCOUNTER

Twenty years had passed between Joseph's sale as a slave to Egypt and the beginning of the worldwide famine. Meanwhile, back at home, Jacob learned that grain was being sold in Egypt. He decided to send his sons to Egypt.

It has been twenty years. Joseph has become the second-in-command in Egypt. Joseph, the one who was hated, mocked, and sold as a slave, is now the one whom everyone needs to call upon to buy grain, unbeknown to them. And his brothers, the mockers, the haters, the schemers, are sitting in a desert tent, wondering where their next meal will come from. Joseph went alone to Egypt and rose to the top. His ten brothers went together to Egypt, hoping to be well-protected, to buy grain. They had no idea what they were about to meet.

Upon arriving in Egypt, all had to bow to Joseph as a sign of honor and respect. Joseph's brothers followed suit and bowed down before him. They had no inkling as to whom they were paying homage to. But Joseph did. He recognized them. Although much older, they kept the same attitude as he remembered from years before. Joseph wasted no time in assuring they got a taste of their own medicine. He spoke roughly to them and asked them where they were from. They responded that they were from Canaan and had come to buy food.

He remembered all the years that he had been deprived of seeing his father and returning home, on account of his brothers' decision to sell him to Egypt. Joseph was now a grown man, not their little helpless brother whom they had treated as a rag doll. Pushing him around, laughing at him, and throwing him into a pit were some of their sports with him. Ignoring his cries to be let out and then pulling him out to get rid of him were actions that demanded justice. Their father never reprimanded them because he had no idea what they had done. They had lied and covered his colored coat with blood so Jacob would believe Joseph had died. They had never received their just dues. Now it was time. Joseph knew what he had to do.

The tables began to turn. Joseph accused them of being spies. They replied that they were not spies. They had come to buy food. They were honest men. Joseph ignored them and accused them of being spies. They then recounted that they were twelve brothers, sons to one man. Their youngest brother had remained with their father, and another had died. Joseph insisted they were spies. He then told them their story would be tested. One of them would be required to return home and bring back their youngest brother, while the rest remained confined in order to prove their story was true. They were imprisoned for three days.

During those three days, his brothers felt a heavy conviction. They had constant memories of the past, memories of the cruel treatment of Joseph, whom they had betrayed. This short isolation period was necessary to prepare their hearts. Their broken relationship was not going to remain that way. God was preparing them all to heal, restore their relationship, and re-establish them.

Despite what had happened between them all those previous years, Joseph genuinely loved them. He feared God and wanted to do things correctly, so he decided to keep one of them, let the others go back with food, and return with the youngest brother to verify their innocence as spies. They agreed.

Without realizing who they were standing before, they discussed their guilt about their brother Joseph. After admitting their guilt, they acknowledged that they were suffering the consequences. Then Reuben accused them all of not listening to him when he had tried to intervene and further reiterated their guilt. This discussion took place within Joseph's hearing because they did not know he understood them. There had been an interpreter between them. He turned away from them and cried.

Joseph was very empathetic. He had suffered so much, and he had not allowed his heart to harden. Even though he spoke roughly to them and let them receive some of their own medicine, it was all done to help his brothers admit their wrongdoings and repent. It was working. He returned and spoke to them. He ordered Simeon to be incarcerated. Then he told his servants to fill each of their bags with grain and to replace each one's money in their sacks. They were provided with provisions for their journey home.

"If your enemy is hungry, give him bread to eat, and if he is thirsty, give him water to drink, for you will heap burning coals on his head, and the Lord will reward you" (Prov 25:21-22).

"Do not be overcome by evil, but overcome evil with good" (Rom 12:21).

"But I say to you who hear, Love your enemies, do good to those who hate you" (Luke 6:27).

They left, and upon arriving at a lodging place, one of them opened his sack to feed his donkey. On top was his money. He showed his brothers. They became fearful as they wondered why the money was there. They began to see the hand of God. When they finally arrived home, they told their father, Jacob, all that had happened in Egypt. They mentioned that the Governor had spoken roughly to them and accused them of being spies. They explained how they tried to defend themselves by telling him that they were twelve brothers, all honest men; one had died, and the youngest had remained in Canaan with their father. They further explained that the man had said that in order to prove that they were honest men, they were to leave one of them with him and the rest return with grain to our household. They were to bring the youngest brother back to him in order to verify that they were not spies. He would release the other brother, and then they would be allowed to trade in the land.

As each man opened their sack, they discovered their money on top of their grain. Jacob and his sons became nervous. Jacob also began to lament. He blamed his sons for his losses. Joseph was gone, Simeon was gone, and now they wanted to take Benjamin. Then Reuben told him to kill his two sons if he did not return Benjamin. He assured him he would bring him back. But Jacob replied that Joseph was dead, and Benjamin was the only one left from Rachel. If he were to lose Benjamin as well, he felt it would mean his death. Jacob clearly underwent a trauma response to all that he had suffered. He experienced many losses and was unwilling to risk another through Benjamin. The pain was too great. He had reached a breaking point.

It seemed as if with each "loss," and by letting go, Jacob was being led to his destiny. If Jacob had known that sending Benjamin to Egypt would have led to his reunion with Joseph, I imagine he would have done so willingly. But all Jacob knew was that Joseph was dead, and his heart was about to be broken again. However, this worldwide famine was going to prove to be the turning point for Jacob and his family's lives.

SEVEN

UNEXPECTED PLEASANTRIES

Over time, the food Jacob's sons had brought from Egypt ran out. The famine had become severe, and their provisions were extremely low. But God had promised that Abraham's descendants would be blessed and be a blessing to others. How could the God who promised Jacob His presence wherever he went allow them to succumb to drought and scarcity? He would not. God would supply for them while all this was happening. It does not matter what is occurring around us. God will always provide and make a way for His own.

Jacob told his sons to return to Egypt to buy more grain. Judah reminded him that they could not return unless they brought Benjamin, the youngest, with them. That was the only way they would be able to buy more grain. The man they were referring to who warned them about returning with Benjamin was none other than Joseph. But they did not know it was him. After much dialogue about the situation, Judah tried once more to convince Jacob to allow Benjamin to go along. He promised he would bear the blame if anything should happen to Benjamin.

Jacob finally relented. He began to prepare some gifts for the man: balm, honey, gum, myrrh, pistachio nuts, and almonds. He recommended they take double the money. That would be the money that they found in their sacks, plus money to buy more grain. He felt it may have been done in error. He then prayed that God would have mercy and allow them all to return safely.

Jacob reached a point of acceptance of the circumstance. He had suffered many losses in life, and now he was being tested to see if he would let go of what was left of his union with Rachel. In his mind, Rachel and Joseph had both died. Now, the only one left, Benjamin, might not return. He was terrified of the thought of never seeing Benjamin again. But he finally gave up what he loved most to save them all.

This moment is similar to an event that happened to his grandfather, Abraham. God had tested Abraham when He asked him to sacrifice his son, Isaac. After waiting for so many years to receive the promised son, he was asked to sacrifice the promise. In the end, Abraham was stopped before he carried it out and sacrificed a ram instead. Now, Jacob was being asked to sacrifice his son for the well-being of the rest of the family. "For God so loved the world, that he gave his only Son, that whoever believes in him should not perish but have eternal life" (John 3:16 ESV). What Jacob feared most, loss, would not happen because he had been tested and had passed each test. He was finally going to see the hand of God. They were about to see the beautiful tapestry that God had been weaving all along. All he had to do was take a step of faith.

Jacob's eleven sons left for Egypt with the gift and double the money. When they arrived, they were taken before Joseph. When Joseph saw Benjamin with them, he ordered his steward to take them to his house and prepare a meal for them as they would be dining with him. When his brothers arrived, they discussed among themselves why they were there. They assumed it was because of the money that they found in their sacks. They thought the man had brought them there to attack them and force them to be his slaves. Remember, they did not know that the man was Joseph. They assumed they were going to receive the same treatment they dished out to Joseph. They were carrying the guilt and condemnation because of their past actions. They remembered their previous visit, how the man spoke roughly to them, and incarcerated them for three days. So, they went to the steward and explained what had happened when they had left the first time, how they had found their money in their sacks, and did not know who put it there. They showed him the extra money they brought to purchase more grain. The steward replied that they should not be afraid. He assured them that he had received their money. He then brought Simeon out to them. He also gave them water to wash their feet and fodder for their donkeys. They were brought into Joseph's house. As they waited, they prepared the gift they had brought. This time, everything was different.

At noontime, when the man arrived, his brothers came before him with their gift and bowed down to him on the ground. Again, remember Joseph's dream, where his brothers bowed down to him. Remember, when they heard the dream, how angry they became? Now, they did it willingly—no complaints on their part. He inquired about their father, if he was still alive and well. They replied that he was alive and well. Such was the love that Joseph had for his father. How much he longed to see him and know that he was well. But he kept himself discreet.

Then he directed his gaze upon Benjamin, his brother, Rachel's son. He asked if this was the youngest brother. With a blessing aimed at his young brother, Joseph quickly exited and entered his quarter to weep. He was overcome with emotion for his brother, whom he had not seen in over twenty years. Here stood the only brother who had been innocent of all the rivalry that he had endured with the rest of his siblings. After washing his face, Joseph then returned to his brothers. After composing himself, he ordered the meal to be served.

The following was the order in which they were seated: Joseph sat at his table, his brothers sat at another table, and the Egyptians, who were part of his household, sat separately.

God had prepared a table for Joseph in the presence of his enemies. "You prepare a table before me in the presence of my enemies; you anoint my head with oil; my cup overflows" (Ps 23:5 ESV). His brothers had made themselves his enemies from his youth, and now they were seeing the table that God had prepared for him apart from them. The Egyptians were also, in a sense, enemies because sitting with the Hebrews was an abomination to them. That is why they sat apart from him and his brothers.

A further observation is that although the Egyptians hated the Hebrews and considered them abominable, it was not that way with Joseph. God had his hand upon Joseph in such a way that the Egyptians looked at him as a god. They revered and respected his authority, and it was only because of God's favor upon his life. He was their savior because he had arrived just in time to save their nation from destruction. Joseph's brothers hated him in his youth because they were jealous of his dreams. They wished it were for them. But it was meant for Joseph because he had been chosen for that position. No one else could handle that role. None of them had endured all that he had, and none of them would have been able to if they had tried. God had proved to all that Joseph was indeed the qualified one. The brothers were seated according to birth order. They looked at each other in amazement, wondering how they knew.

Portions from Joseph's table were served to his brothers, but Benjamin received five times as much as any of them. Joseph showed his love and compassion towards his brothers by sharing his blessings with them without revealing who he really was. Even in such a prominent position, Joseph displayed a humble spirit. His brothers, without knowing it was Joseph, felt an ease and peaceful environment that they were able to enjoy this meal together with him. I cannot reiterate how this moment could only be achieved by the grace of God. It was a small beginning and evidence of a profound healing that was taking place. And yet, there remained a final test that would reveal the hearts of each of them.

EIGHT

CONFRONTATION

At the end of the meal, Joseph told his household steward to fill the men's sacks with as much food as they could carry, as well as the money they had brought to pay for the grain. In addition, he instructed him to place not only the youngest brother's money in his sack but Joseph's silver cup as well. The steward followed Joseph's instructions.

The following morning, they arose early and began their journey home. When they were only a short distance away, Joseph told his steward to follow the men and ask them why they had repaid evil for good and why they would steal the cup that he drank and practiced divination from. To accuse them of doing evil.

When the steward overtook them, he told them these things. They responded and asked him why he was saying such words. They reminded him that they had brought back the money that had been placed in their sacks without their knowledge and asked how it was possible that they could steal silver or gold from his lord's house. They then declared that whoever was found with the silver cup would die, and the rest would remain as servants. The steward agreed but said that in whosoever's sack the silver cup was found would stay as a servant, and the rest would be free.

After dismounting their donkeys, the men began opening their sacks for the steward to view. He started with the eldest and continued with each. The cup was found in the youngest's sack, that of Benjamin. They tore their clothes in grief, remounted their donkeys, and headed back to the city.

Upon arriving at Joseph's house, Judah and his brothers fell before him to the ground. Joseph asked them what deed was it that they had done; did they not know that he could practice divination?

Judah responded, "What can we say? How can we clear our name?" Then, he finally acknowledged that God had uncovered their guilt. The brothers were all willing to be Joseph's servants.

Although the appearance of the silver cup in Benjamin's sack triggered their guilt, they still had not acknowledged the actual reason for their guilt.

Joseph then pushed them further by saying that only the one in whose sack the silver cup had been found would be his servant, and the rest were free to return to their home. The brothers became distraught, and Judah asked to speak.

He recounted the events from the first time they arrived in Egypt to buy grain. Joseph had asked them if they had a father or another brother. They replied that they had an elderly father and a younger brother born in his old age. His brother had died, and he was the only one left of his mother's children, and he was beloved of his father. Joseph then requested to see him, but they responded that they could not bring him because their father would not be able to handle it; he would die. Joseph then insisted they get him and bring him before him. Otherwise, they would not be able to buy any grain.

Judah continued and told him that when they returned to their home, they told their father what had happened. He had refused to send Benjamin. Then, he asked them to return to Egypt to buy more grain. They explained to him again that they could not return without Benjamin. Jacob, their father, responded that his wife had birthed two children. The first was no more and was never seen again, killed by an animal. If they were to take Benjamin and something were to happen to him, he said he would die.

Judah continued by saying that if they returned to their father without Benjamin, he would be devastated and die, and they would bear the blame for his death. Judah explained that he had promised his father to bring Benjamin back, and if not, he would bear the blame forever. Judah pleaded with Joseph to allow him to remain as his servant and allow Benjamin to return to his father. He said he could not face his father without Benjamin, knowing that it would kill him.

NINE

THE BIG REVEAL

Judah and his brothers were backed against the wall. What they had avoided for over twenty years had come and stared at them in the face. They could not move in any direction because they were blocked from doing so. Let me explain.

After so many years of jealousy and hatred towards Joseph, they had schemed to get rid of him and make him disappear so as never to have to deal with him again. At first, the plan to kill him was too obvious. That would have been permanent, and they reasoned that it would have meant they would carry blood on their hands. So, they came up with a better idea. Sell him to traders. They not only would erase him from their midst, but they would be free from blood guilt. After they sold him to the Midianite traders, they decided to divert their guilt to a wild animal. They killed a goat from their father's flock and dipped Joseph's coat in it to show that an animal had killed him. They carried out their goal: Joseph was gone, and they did not have to kill him themselves; "an animal" had done it. Upon presenting Joseph's coat to Jacob, he believed their story. Joseph had been killed. Jacob went into a depression and lost all his vigor and energy for life. Although Joseph was alive, he was hurled into a myriad of hardships and injustices that spanned over many years. Therefore, his sons destroyed Joseph and Jacob, causing them much suffering for over twenty years. Because of their unresolved jealousy and hatred issues, they selfishly chose to ruin their bloodline.

Had it not been for God's intervention, Jacob and Joseph would have died. All of that was not enough to sabotage God's plan and purpose.

Joseph's character was revealed in his behavior towards his brothers. His rough treatment of them was necessary. Their conduct towards both Jacob and Joseph showed their lack of familial honor. They had no respect for anyone until now. Joseph was no longer a young teenager nor a weak bully magnet. He had grown into a great man, full of strength, wisdom, and purpose. He was a prime minister with authority and a whole army at his disposal to defend him if necessary. His brothers were on his royal territory, seeking mercy and bread to eat. They were the helpless ones now. The tables had turned, and now they had no choice but to accept whatever justice would be wielded at them.

With all this in mind, let us return to the story.

As Judah related the events that had occurred up to this moment, Joseph's demeanor began to change. His empathy and compassion began to surface. He could no longer hide his identity. He sent all his servants out and remained alone with his brothers. He wept aloud, so much so that even the Pharaoh and many Egyptians heard him.

He then told his brothers plainly, "I am Joseph! Is my father still alive?" They all stood with their mouths agape, speechless, and unable to move. It was an unexpected moment, the biggest surprise they had ever received. The range of emotions they experienced in that moment was too much for them to understand and process. Joseph called for them to draw closer, and they did. He continued.

"So, Joseph said to his brothers, 'Come near to me, please." And they came near. And he said, "I am your brother, Joseph, whom you sold into Egypt. And now do not be distressed or angry with yourselves because you sold me here, for God sent me before you to preserve life. For the famine has been in the land these two years, and there are yet five years in which there will be neither plowing nor harvest. And God sent me before you to preserve for you a remnant on earth, and to keep alive for you many survivors. So, it was not you who sent me here, but God. He has made me a father to Pharaoh, and Lord of all his house and ruler over all the land of Egypt" (Gen 45:4-8). These words helped his brothers understand what God had been doing all along. Joseph, as a ruler of Egypt, was going to help them all. He was their savior. The one they had despised and hated was the one who would preserve their lives and be a blessing to them. It was all God's doing. In one instance, each of their hearts was changed. They looked at Joseph with love, honor, and respect. Their "little brother" was their hero.

After a long weeping session, hugs, and a heart-to-heart chat, he instructed them to return home and share everything with their father. They were to let him know that Joseph was alive and the ruler of Egypt. His father was to come down to live in the best of Egypt, the land of Goshen: the whole family, all the children, grandchildren, the flocks, the herds, and all their possessions. All their needs would be met because there were yet five years of famine left to endure. They were to let him know that it was indeed Joseph; they had seen him with their own eyes.

At the palace, the Pharaoh was informed that Joseph's brothers had come, which pleased him and his servants. The Pharaoh directed Joseph to tell his brothers to load up their donkeys, return to their land, and bring their father and the rest of the family to Egypt. The Pharaoh assured them he would give them the best of the land and that they would be well taken care of. He also told Joseph to tell them to take wagons from Egypt for the little children, their wives, and their father to travel. They were not to be concerned about anything because they were going to enjoy the best of what Egypt had to offer.

Such was God's favor in Joseph's life. Pharaoh himself opened his heart to receive Joseph's family from the land of Canaan out of love and appreciation. He knew God had sent Joseph to save his people and the rest of the world during this worldwide crisis. He offered the best for them. Who does that? This royal treatment was clearly the hand of God.

Joseph went ahead and gave his brothers the wagons and plenty of provisions for their trip. He gave each of them a change of clothes, but to Benjamin, he gave three hundred shekels of silver and five changes of clothing. He sent his father ten donkeys loaded with good things from Egypt and ten female donkeys loaded with grain, bread, and provisions for his father throughout his trip. His brothers set off on their way, and Joseph's parting shot for them was to not quarrel along the way.

The amount of time each trip took depended on the number of people, the weather conditions, whether there were many animals, etc. Joseph would have to wait several months, perhaps because of the number of people traveling, which included women and children, and all the herds and flocks of animals. Their rate of travel had to be slower. They had to rest and spend the night wherever they found themselves on their journey. With all these factors considered, one can only imagine the level of apprehension he felt in the waiting. He could only trust in God to bring them all safely.

Upon arriving in Canaan, his brothers relayed the message to Jacob that Joseph was alive and ruler over all of Egypt. His heart became numb, as if in a state of shock. It was much too unbelievable for him to process. After so many years, he had already accepted that Joseph was dead, and he would never see him again. To now hear that Joseph was indeed alive was beyond his comprehension. Seeing the wagons loaded with provisions, and hearing one son after another verifying it helped him to believe and decide that he would move quickly to see his son before he died. His spirit revived, and after dealing with a period of twenty years of hopelessness and despair, he felt hope and faith take hold of his heart. There was joy and a celebratory spirit in the camp as everyone excitedly packed to begin their travel to Egypt. Many were eager to see Joseph finally, and even more, as Prime Minister of Egypt. But none more than Jacob.

TEN

REUNION AND A FINAL GOODBYE

Jacob began his journey with his family and all his possessions to Egypt. They rested in Beersheba and offered sacrifices to God. God spoke to him in a vision at night. After telling him not to fear going down to Egypt, He reminded him of His promise that He would make him a great nation. He also reassured Jacob that He would go with Him and bring him back up again, and that Joseph would be the one to close his eyes, meaning Joseph would be by his side at his time of death. Knowing that Joseph was alive and waiting for him in Egypt was a comfort to Jacob.

Jacob left Beersheba and continued his journey. His sons carried their father, women, and children in the wagons that the Pharaoh had sent. Everything they possessed, their herds, and all the members of their family traveled. The total number of persons who arrived in Egypt, excluding Jacob's sons' wives, was sixty-six. Adding Joseph's two sons, Joseph and Jacob, made a total of 70 people who came to Egypt.

Jacob sent Judah ahead to prepare the way for his arrival in Goshen, the land that the Pharaoh had appointed for them. Meanwhile, Joseph prepared his chariot to meet his father in Goshen. At their reunion, Joseph came before him, and they embraced and wept for a long while. There was incredible peace and happiness, finally, as both father and son came together after so many years of separation. The longing, the pain, and the sorrow were now only a memory as they began their journey of life together once again.

Joseph had to prepare his family for their transition into their new life in Goshen. He presented his brothers before the king and informed him of their occupation as shepherds, which was an abomination to the Egyptians. God's favor on Joseph's life allowed the Egyptians to bypass many of their prejudices. As they began their acclimation, the Pharaoh asked that anyone capable among them be put in charge of his livestock.

Joseph presented Jacob to the king. The Pharaoh inquired about his age, and Jacob replied that he was 130 years old and that it was not close to his father's years. After pronouncing a blessing upon the Pharaoh, Jacob left his presence.

Joseph had a lot on his plate. As Prime Minister, he had many duties to attend to and now also had to settle his family into the land. He made sure they received their provision of food supply as part of the arrangement.

During the five years that remained, the famine became very severe in all the land of Egypt and Canaan. For this reason, Joseph gathered all the money found in Egypt and Canaan in exchange for the purchase of the grain. The money was placed in the treasury of the king's palace. Without money, the Egyptians had no way to buy grain. They came before Joseph and begged for grain since they had no money left. Joseph told them to exchange their livestock. So, they brought their horses, flocks, herds, and donkeys. He was able to supply them with enough food for another year. The following year, they came before Joseph and again requested grain, explaining they had no money, no herds, or flocks, but only their land and their physical bodies. They were in an extreme crisis, and the only recourse or action was to sell themselves and their land to the king in order to survive.

Joseph's position required wisdom and vision from only God above. Although the world's population was much less than it is presently, to be able to supply food to the world at even that time was a tall order. Every year required a different approach. Joseph had to keep reaching high for a new level of understanding simply because this was something that had never happened before. Everyone, even the king, was looking to him for the answers to this crisis, and God provided the means to carry out the survival of humanity during that time.

Joseph bought all the land of Egypt for the Pharaoh. As for the people, he made them servants, as he had bought them and their land for the Pharaoh. He then provided them with seeds to sow the land. They were to give a fifth of their harvests to Pharaoh and keep four-fifths for themselves. This amount would provide food for them and seeds for further sowing. With gratitude to Joseph for saving their lives, the people were willing to be servants to Pharaoh.

Israel settled in the land of Goshen in Egypt. They got possessions and grew and multiplied exceedingly. Jacob lived an additional seventeen years, for a total of one hundred forty-seven years. As his days were drawing nearer to his death, he made Joseph promise that he would not bury him in Egypt. Jacob wanted to be buried with his ancestors in Canaan. Joseph pledged and assured him that he would do so. During his final days, Jacob blessed Joseph's sons. As in his case with his brother Esau, the same prophecy that the elder would serve the younger was applied. Ephraim was put before Manasseh and promised the blessing of the firstborn. Later, Jacob's sons gathered around him, and their father gave each a prophecy and blessing. Jacob then gave them instructions for his burial. Shortly thereafter, Jacob passed away. It is incredible to see how God allowed Jacob to set everything in order before his death.

Joseph mourned deeply the loss of his father, as he loved him greatly. He asked permission from the Pharaoh to bury his father in Canaan in a specific cave in Machpelah, east of Mamre, that his grandfather, Abraham, had bought. There, Abraham, Sarah, Isaac, and Rebecca were buried. With Pharaoh's consent, Joseph and his brothers, their families, Pharaoh's servants, the elders of his household, and chariots and horse riders all went with Joseph to lay Jacob in his final resting place. There, they gathered for seven days in such grievous mourning that the inhabitants of that region took notice. Upon completion of this final act of respect towards Jacob by his family and loved ones, they all returned to Egypt.

ELEVEN

SURPRISE ENDING AND KINDNESS

The Scriptures do not specify an amount of time, but one day, Joseph's brothers spoke among themselves about whether Joseph might punish them now that their father was dead. They honestly thought that Joseph was vindictive and had waited seventeen years to finally exact revenge upon them. This mindset was what set them apart from Joseph. They still felt guilty and decided to come up with a solution to their dilemma. They cooked up a lie in order to protect themselves. They went with a message to Joseph, saying that their father had commanded them to ask Joseph to forgive them for all they had done to him. They pleaded with him to forgive the transgressions of the servants of the God of their father. Joseph's reaction was unexpected. He wept when he heard these words. His humility just added more of a sense of guilt because they fell before him and declared they were his servants.

Joseph told them not to be afraid. What he said next was the key that had already unlocked the door to his elevation and success. "But Joseph said to them, "Do not fear, for am I in the place of God? As for you, you meant evil against me, but God meant it for good, to bring it about that many people should be kept alive, as they are today. So do not fear; I will provide for you and your little ones." Thus he comforted them and spoke kindly to them" (Genesis 50:19-21).

Joseph's mindset was brilliant. He had elevated to such a point that he could see beyond what others could not. In that journey and period of isolation, God had freed him to see his purpose. It was God who had been in his ear, revealing His plan to him all along. He was no longer a victim of the circumstances that others had placed him in. His response revealed the transformation God had wrought in him.

Joseph could see that, despite the evil treatment he had received from others, God had used all of it to bring about his dreams. It did not stop his movement towards his destiny. No one could destroy him because God was the driving force pushing him into his position. Even though, in human terms, it took a long time, that time was insignificant to God. Time had been used to prepare Joseph, so it did not matter how long it took; Joseph was right on time. It all aligned with the time of the worldwide famine. He had had seven years of preparing for it during the years of abundance. God downloaded to him the instructions to make it through the years of want. Joseph chose to forgive his brothers and secured freedom from bitterness and resentment. His brothers, on the contrary, did not understand because they did not see it that way until he explained it to them. It was only then that their eyes were opened, and they were able to receive that forgiveness and be at peace with him. He continued treating them with love and kindness and made sure their needs were met.

Before his death at the age of 110, Joseph prophesied that God would bring them back to the land He had promised to Abraham, Isaac, and Jacob. He made the sons of Israel promise that when that time arrived, they would take his bones back with them. He was buried in a coffin in Egypt. That prophecy came about during the Exodus, and that generation led by Moses fulfilled that request.

TWELVE

THE GIST OF THE MATTER

Many people have suffered at the hands of a bully, narcissist, or toxic person at some point in their lives. Some have gone on to heal and thrive despite those hardships and adversities, while others have never been able to move on. To all these Josephs, I dedicate this chapter with a message of hope and inspiration.

I never thought of myself as Joseph. I did not even know that it was possible. After studying his life and his impact on humanity during his time, I started to reflect on my own life. I began to remember my firsthand experiences and discovered that, although there are parts of my life I would like to forget, they are a part of me that I cannot erase. They played a role in who I am today.

Without getting into much detail, I will share some painful moments from my past so you can understand where I am coming from. Perhaps we share common ground.

I recall feeling lost as a child when I was placed in a school setting or an unfamiliar environment. I felt unprepared to deal with others because it seemed as if everyone knew what to do, but I did not know. There were times when I was humiliated, made fun of, threatened, intimidated, and bullied. In kindergarten, a student pulled down my pants. As I quickly pulled them up, I struggled with a feeling called humiliation. This episode would repeat many times through my life in different formats. When I was eight years old, I was molested by an older family member. That was a devastating moment because I felt like a part of my childhood was taken away by someone whom I looked up to. I was threatened not to tell, and this family member never apologized. During that same time, I remember an incident that happened when I was in third grade, as I was heading home at the end of the school day. A boy in my class called me bad names from a distance; I honestly do not know why. So, I said to him, No, you. He came up to me and slapped me across the face. I ran home, threw myself on my bed, and cried. The next day, my sister went with me to the principal's office and told him about it, and the boy was at once reprimanded.

During my middle school years, a male student bullied me for three years. I told my teacher, but nothing was ever done. It crushed my self-esteem because he mocked my physical appearance. I did not know how to stand up for myself, so I stayed quiet. But deep down inside, I felt so broken. No one ever stood up for me. I also had some female relatives who constantly criticized my body shape during that period of my life as well. Every time they saw me they made sure that I knew that I was imperfect. My mom eventually commented to them how that made me feel bad about myself. They responded that they did not think I felt that way. Some people called me dumb for not responding.

These constant attacks set me up for years of feeling inferior to everyone else. They achieved their goal for many years of my life. I did not know any better. I questioned what I had done that would cause them to feel the liberty to treat me that way. I never treated anyone that way, so I did not understand. I came across people who said things to make me feel dumb. Name-calling, mockery, and rude comments were often made in public to humiliate me. It was not till I had grown and come to realize this: these toxic individuals who deliberately created situations to provoke a reaction in me hid behind their negativity by projecting their insecurities onto me. I did not understand that behavior because I did not think that way about people. I never intentionally tried to bring someone down to make myself feel better. That was and is still an alien concept to me. Since I had a religious upbringing, I knew the golden rule- "Do unto others as you would like them to do unto you." I learned that you should treat others with kindness and respect, irrespective of the status or appearance of the person. But as time passed, I began to understand a concept called toxicity in society. It is a poison that has the potential to destroy lives.

To be clear, I had many wonderful moments during those same years that I remember fondly and am grateful for. I had a few close friends whose friendship I will always treasure. Certain people in my life were mentors who reached out to me with kindness and love. God always provided someone to help me get through those difficult moments.

Within society, there exists the pure-hearted and the bully. The pure-hearted get attacked, mistreated, and abused. The bully cannot stand to see the pure-hearted who, although imperfect, do good to others. It is like they have a radar, and on the screen, it says "destroy." They are professionals at it and have no trouble carrying out that goal. Whereas the pure-hearted's radar says "love." They also have no problem loving others and do it almost effortlessly. Neither group fully understands the other's behavior.

Despite presenting themselves as superior and tough, bullies are weak and very insecure. Their mindset tells them that anyone who cares, shows kindness and compassion, and gives generously without expecting in return is weak. They think that belittling, mocking, intimidating, threatening, attacking, gaslighting, accusing, and smearing their target will somehow keep them discouraged, overwhelmed, and oppressed. To be clear, everyone has a purpose in life. These bullies have failed to discover theirs. They spend their days in these attack campaigns, and in the process, their life passes by, causing them misery. It does not occur to them to find their purpose and enjoy their life in fulfilling it.

I believe their main objective is to humiliate the target. Humiliation rituals are an everyday occurrence in society. They do not discriminate based on status- either gender, young or old, and the wealthy can be subjected to them. I have even seen religious individuals think it is necessary to humble people they believe need it. If we follow the Bible, it does not instruct us to humble others. It says humble yourself.

"Humble yourselves before the Lord, and he will exalt you" (James 4:10).

"Humble yourselves, therefore, under the mighty hand of God so that at the proper time he may exalt you," (1 Peter 5:6).

"For everyone who exalts himself will be humbled, and he who humbles himself will be exalted" (Luke 14:11).

(If you, my friend, believe it necessary to humble others, please stop. God is not pleased.)

Bullies often have the idea that the pure-hearted are proud or arrogant because they do not show many insecurities. They may seem confident, and this confidence triggers the bully, who lacks confidence. Why is this? The bully lives under constant guilt. They know what they are doing is wrong, so they bear their guilt, which makes them insecure. The pure-hearted are confident because they are not doing evil things to others. Therefore, they walk securely. They are at peace with themselves and others.

I believe the pure-hearted are here as teachers. They are insightful, and they bring profound truth to the mediocre and the bullies. Each should try to evolve. According to Proverbs 6:16-19 (New Living Translation)- "There are six things the Lord hates- no, seven things he detests: haughty eyes, a lying tongue, hands that kill the innocent, a heart that plots evil, feet that race to do wrong, a false witness that pours out lies, a person who sows discord in a family." Many of these actions are rooted in jealousy and envy, which should lead us to keep our hearts in check.

It is interesting that in the Beatitudes, found in Matthew 5, the pure in heart are promised that they shall see God. Throughout Joseph's life, we read that God was with Joseph. Joseph pleased God because of his heart posture. He had no possessions, no degree, no fame, or worldly acclaim, yet it pleased God to choose him to rise as a savior to the world because of his pure heartedness. (I am not referring to the Savior, Jesus Christ, who, while sinless, was the only one who could fulfill the redemption of humankind.)

Merely an enslaved person in an Egyptian prison, he surpassed all the wise counselors, the royal officials, and the Pharaoh's upper class. As it says in 1 Samuel 16:7b- "The Lord does not look at the things people look at. People look at the outward appearance, but the Lord looks at the heart." The crisis was to be handled by God through his servant Joseph. Everything he went through in his life prepared him for this mission. The incredible mental strength he received during those years of suffering prepared him for the assignment before him. His character was unmatched by those in the king's court. Pharaoh saw the wisdom and understanding Joseph had. He was qualified.

Joseph was teachable, which enabled him to achieve wisdom and knowledge. While his brothers tended to be reckless and rebellious, Joseph supported an obedient heart toward authority and a willingness to learn and grow. He was an observant thinker and passed every test life threw at him. God knew Joseph was reliable. The many years he spent in prison were proportionate to the extent of his calling.

God is patient. He foreknew all the events that Joseph would have to pass through, and there was never a moment when Joseph was delayed in his purpose. Everything occurred with precision. That is encouraging for those who struggle with the waiting period before receiving their promises from God. God did not forget about Joseph during those years in prison. He was with Joseph and made sure Joseph entered his position at the right time. God does not forget any of His children. He is always on time.

Joseph's dreams were fulfilled only by God's work, which was happening behind the scenes. All Joseph had to do was continue his daily tasks, even when they were mundane and even dull. He probably never realized he was being watched and admired by the others in that prison. Why? Because Joseph feared God. He did not complain, he did not speak evil, and he did not waste his time trying to fit in. God's plan will always prevail. It did not matter what anyone may have thought about Joseph. It did not matter who may have tried to block his blessing. God removed each and continued to lead Joseph to his place of honor and rule. For that was his purpose. Once he was called out of prison, his life was never the same. Joseph's enemies and accusers were present when his dream was fulfilled. Even Potiphar's wife had to bow before the one she had falsely accused, as well as Joseph's brothers. There was no room for doubt that God set Joseph on the throne in the second command in Egypt. When God has called you to a particular purpose or position, the haters and the manipulators will not succeed in stopping you. They may throw whatever they can at you, they may smear you, and these individuals may try to block you, but God will walk you right through it. You can be sure you will reach your destiny.

The wait and patience were the required currency. The many years in preparation were the price for his crown. Many want to be placed in a position of authority but do not want to pass through the years of preparation. The call to leadership by God is not just a degree. It is not who you know or your connections. It is not how many followers you may have. It is not your wealth. It begins in the heart, which will be tested in many ways. It is after the testing that God places His certificate of high-grade test, His seal of approval, and His mark of genuineness.

There is a similarity between Jesus Christ and Joseph that cannot be ignored. Both were hated and despised by their brethren. However, in Jesus' case, it was the Pharisees who were representatives of his Israelite brethren. Both Jesus and Joseph were chosen to save their people. They suffered persecution and betrayal. They were faithful to their call. They ultimately reached their position to fulfill the call of the savior. Jesus Christ died on the cross to save humanity from their sins and provide eternal life. Joseph was taken out of prison and placed in a place of prominence to give food to the masses during the famine; he saved them from certain death.

Being like Jesus is the highest compliment anyone can ever receive. Every believer/Christian should strive to be like Jesus. Many people expect this from those who claim to be followers of Christ. There is no room for the fakery. It does matter what you may claim; your life must back up your words and your posts. Look at what God's Word says in Matthew 7:21: "Not everyone who says to Me, 'Lord, Lord,' shall enter the kingdom of heaven, but he who does the will of My Father in heaven." We must be more concerned with what God thinks about us than with what others think.

Joseph and Jesus both demonstrated a love for others and care for their well-being. They did not see skin color, race, social status, age, or even gender as a factor to exclude anyone when helping them. God did a miracle in Egypt because the Egyptians were racist against the Hebrews. They did not tolerate them at all. But God brought a Hebrew to them and taught them to accept and love them during Joseph's reign. They loved Joseph to the point that they did whatever he asked. That is what love does in people's lives. God ended prejudice among them, and there was unity and camaraderie. My friend, I invite you to be willing to see others through God's eyes and remove any prejudice you may have towards others who are unlike you.

I cannot emphasize enough that everyone has a purpose, no matter how small or insignificant, and needs to work on it. We are imperfect, but we can grow and become better with patience, persistence, and faithfulness. With God, all things are possible.

There is always the possibility that a person we meet at some point may hold the answer to our problem and be the provider of a particular need. We would do well to maintain respect for others because it is the right thing to do.

A couple of years ago, I was at a low point in my life. I was not involved in any risky behavior; instead, I was involved in church. But my situation was very complicated. I was in a marriage with the wrong person. For twenty years, I was with someone who had cheated and sabotaged me, and although we had enough material wealth, there was constant discord. We had four children. There was no peace. I felt sick, and I felt like my life was going downhill fast. I do not know if anyone around me knew what was happening, but no one ever said anything. It got to the point that I knew I could no longer continue in that marriage. I spoke with my ex and let them know how I felt. They did not express anything that showed a desire to work on the marriage, which led me to understand that there was nothing to try to salvage in that relationship. There were many other factors that I will not get into that also contributed to the break-up.

I filed for divorce and received custody of my two youngest. I began to practice self-care. I looked online and found many resources to help me through this process. Every day was another step towards my healing process. I pushed through even when I faced moments of discouragement. I cried many tears, but it felt like I was shedding layers of me that no longer fit who I was becoming. I had hope again. Although I had no one to help me, I pressed on. The reality is God was with me through it all. He provided the resources, and everything I needed. In the moments when I felt overwhelmed, He was there, comforting me. This process was long because of the number of years that I had endured silent suffering.

After nearly a year and a half, I was able to move to another state and officially begin my new life. It took living one day at a time to allow me the time I needed to heal and discover who I was. My identity had been covered up by others' opinions and control over my life. For example, I was free to dress how I wanted without being judged by anyone. I began enjoying the hobbies that I liked. I felt free to be me and not have to fit in. I did not look at others' expressions to decide whether I was doing the right thing. All this happened in an isolated environment. It taught me boundaries. I learned to love who I was and accept myself. No longer would I allow anyone to abuse and disrespect me. I began to experience peace, joy, and love to an extent I never had. I smiled more and felt comfortable when I was out in public. I could look at others in the eyes without feeling ashamed.

What I learned about myself was found in the Word of God. I learned how much He loved me, that I was His daughter, and that He had a plan and purpose for my life. He showed me that despite my mistakes, He could still use them for my good. It was such a relief to know my value came from God and not others. God knew my heart and intentions and was the only one qualified to judge me. Knowing my purpose, gifts, abilities, and skills allowed me to focus on my purpose and not enter into competitiveness with others. I could admire others and not feel envy or jealousy, which is common nowadays.

After so many years of questioning the whys concerning the abuse and humiliation I endured, I finally understood that I had internalized what others had done to me. That was the manipulation they had tethered to me. I had allowed shame and fear to dominate me. Now, I realize that I was not to blame for their treatment of me. I did not do anything to deserve this treatment, and I removed shame from my life. I now wear a new garment of royalty as a daughter of the King of Kings. All this is for the glory of God.

I cannot associate or bring everyone into the circle of my life. My circle is small. Not because I cannot forgive the betrayers, the abusers, the gossipers, and the manipulators. I have forgiven them. But my life is different. I do not participate in those activities. They were the ones who wanted to destroy me. Why would I go back to that? God pulled me out and brought me into a better place. 1 Corinthians 15:33- "Do not be deceived: 'Bad company ruins good character.'" Psalm 141:4- "Do not let my heart incline to any evil, to busy myself with wicked deeds in company with men who work iniquity and let me not eat of their delicacies!"

To all the Josephs struggling with rejection, betrayal, manipulation, and bullying, you can be sure that God sees and wants to not only heal your wounds but walk with you into your purpose. He loves you so much. When you accept the Lord into your life, you begin a new life as a new creation in Christ, as stated in 2 Corinthians 5:17. All your sins are forgiven; you have a clean slate. Everything becomes new. You carry a new identity that is found in Christ. You will be a child of God. The healing will begin, and you will discover your purpose. Life will take on new meaning. Your desires will change. Your focus will be on a satisfying and fulfilled life. You will experience the perfect love of God that you never had, a peace that passes all understanding, and a joy unspeakable. Does that mean you will never face difficulties or problems in life? No, but you will have God on your side, leading you and giving you the strength that you will need to face any challenge along the way.

As Joseph met many obstacles and battles, you will also face challenges. With God by your side, you will face each one and overcome them. Every giant trying to get you off course will be overthrown. It is a daily process, but you are guaranteed to win.

1 John 5:4 states: "For whatsoever is born of God overcometh the world: and this is the victory that overcometh the world, even our faith."

There is one significant challenge you will face that many people struggle with, and that is forgiving those who have hurt you. Forgiveness is mandatory to heal. Colossians 3:13b states, "Forgiving each other, as the Lord has forgiven you, so you also must forgive." We must forgive as our Heavenly Father has forgiven us. It has nothing to do with whether the person deserves it. Forgiving will cause you to avoid the root of bitterness from taking root in your heart. Bitterness will block you from progressing, from growing, from the blessings of God. As you forgive, you will experience freedom. Forgiveness is an act of the will; it is not based on feelings. It is based on your willingness to forgive despite how you feel. Forgiveness cannot depend on feelings because feelings will never want to forgive.

As you leave the past behind, focus on the present, and decide to forgive, your life will improve, and you will be able to achieve the goals and purposes of your life. It is impossible to erase the memories of the past, but it is possible to focus on the present and the future. As you create new memories to enjoy, you will no longer be a prisoner of the past but be free to appreciate life in the present and the future. Forgiveness is the key to freedom.

Forgiveness also means allowing God to remove the associations that want to continue to destroy you. You keep them at a distance. You can pray for them and wish them well, but you are not obligated to accept them back into your life. You must pray and let God guide you, for He alone knows people's hearts and their intentions towards you. I say this because they may see the wonderful blessings God has for you and try to come back in in order to partake of those very blessings. Those blessings are yours, not for them. He cannot honor those who continue to intentionally hurt others. They must go to Him and repent. Some may become malicious and smear you. Let them. God sees everything. Again, pray and let God direct you. God may allow someone to come because they did repent.

As in Joseph's case, each disappointment propelled him to a new position of authority, in part due to his willingness to forgive and let go. Joseph was able to withstand and overcome every challenge and obstacle that stood in his way. He did not allow the setbacks to hinder him but used them as steppingstones to move forward to his purpose. Joseph had no room for hate because the Lord was with him and had filled his heart with love. As previously mentioned, it is not always possible to stay in a relationship with an enemy if they are not willing to change. Still, it is possible to forgive and move on.

There is an important question that should be asked. Did God fulfill his plan and purpose for Joseph? It is an obvious yes. Joseph's dreams came to fruition, without fail. Joseph did not ask or dream up those dreams out of his own will. They came directly from God. Therefore, since God was the originator, He had to see it through. He is not a liar, nor a deceiver. He spoke it and it came to pass. It is no less for you and me if we have a dream from God. We can be sure that whatever he has promised, He will be sure to carry it out.

To you, my friend, who has had your share of suffering and pain, I offer you a warm hug, prayer, and encouragement. The trials and sorrows you are facing or have faced will not last forever. As you heal, there will be good days and complicated days. You have permission to be human. Just remember, if you have God, you have it all. Trust in Him, for He will never fail you.

Isaiah 41:10-13 offers a promise of hope for you if you commit yourself to Him. "Fear not, for I am with you; be not dismayed for I am your God; I will strengthen you, I will help you, I will uphold you with my righteous right hand. Behold, all who are incensed against you shall be put to shame and confounded; those who strive against you shall be as nothing and shall perish. You shall seek those who contend with you, but you shall not find them; those who war against you shall be as nothing as all. For I, the Lord your God, hold your right hand; it is I who say to you, "Fear not, I am the one who helps you."

www.ingramcontent.com/pod-product-compliance
Lightning Source LLC
Chambersburg PA
CBHW081254040426
42453CB00014B/2407